50 Italian Pasta Variety Recipes for Home

By: Kelly Johnson

Table of Contents

- Spaghetti Carbonara
- Fettuccine Alfredo
- Penne Arrabbiata
- Linguine with Clam Sauce
- Ravioli with Sage Butter Sauce
- Lasagna Bolognese
- Tagliatelle with Pesto Genovese
- Gnocchi alla Sorrentina
- Farfalle with Creamy Mushroom Sauce
- Cannelloni Ricotta e Spinaci
- Orecchiette with Broccoli Rabe and Sausage
- Tortellini in Brodo (Tortellini in Broth)
- Spaghetti alla Puttanesca
- Rigatoni alla Norma
- Pappardelle with Wild Boar Ragu
- Conchiglie with Tomato and Basil Sauce
- Paccheri with Seafood
- Cacio e Pepe
- Bucatini all'Amatriciana
- Aglio e Olio (Garlic and Olive Oil Pasta)
- Strozzapreti with Pancetta and Peas
- Cavatelli with Broccoli and Sausage
- Manicotti alla Fiorentina
- Fusilli with Roasted Vegetables
- Pici with Tuscan Sausage Sauce
- Tortellini alla Panna
- Mezze Maniche with Gorgonzola Sauce
- Spaghetti alla Nerano
- Farfalle with Smoked Salmon and Cream Sauce
- Ravioli di Zucca (Pumpkin Ravioli)
- Fettuccine with Shrimp Scampi
- Penne alla Vodka
- Linguine with Lobster Sauce
- Lasagna Verde
- Tagliatelle with Truffle Cream Sauce

- Gnocchi alla Romana
- Farfalle with Asparagus and Prosciutto
- Cannelloni al Forno
- Orecchiette with Broccoli and Anchovies
- Spaghetti alla Siciliana
- Rigatoni con Pesto Trapanese
- Pappardelle with Rabbit Ragu
- Conchiglie alla Fiorentina
- Paccheri with Eggplant and Ricotta Salata
- Cacio e Pepe with Lemon Zest
- Bucatini with Tuna and Capers
- Strozzapreti with Cherry Tomatoes and Burrata
- Cavatelli with Rapini and Garlic
- Manicotti with Ricotta and Spinach
- Fusilli with Pistachio Pesto

Spaghetti Carbonara

Ingredients:

- 350g spaghetti
- 150g pancetta or guanciale, diced
- 3 large eggs
- 100g Pecorino Romano cheese, grated (plus extra for serving)
- Freshly ground black pepper
- Salt (for pasta water)
- Optional: chopped parsley for garnish

Instructions:

1. Bring a large pot of salted water to a boil. Cook the spaghetti according to package instructions until al dente. Reserve about 1 cup of pasta water before draining.
2. While the pasta is cooking, heat a large skillet over medium heat. Add the diced pancetta or guanciale and cook until crispy and golden brown, about 5-7 minutes. Remove from heat and set aside.
3. In a mixing bowl, whisk together the eggs, grated Pecorino Romano cheese, and a generous amount of freshly ground black pepper until well combined.
4. Once the pasta is cooked, drain it and immediately transfer it to the skillet with the cooked pancetta or guanciale. Toss the pasta with the pancetta/guanciale to coat.
5. Quickly pour the egg and cheese mixture over the hot pasta while continuously tossing the pasta to coat it evenly. The residual heat from the pasta will cook the eggs and melt the cheese, creating a creamy sauce. If the sauce is too thick, you can add a bit of the reserved pasta water to loosen it up.
6. Once the sauce has coated the pasta and reached a creamy consistency, divide the spaghetti carbonara among serving plates. Sprinkle with additional grated Pecorino Romano cheese and chopped parsley, if desired. Serve immediately.

Enjoy your delicious homemade Spaghetti Carbonara!

Fettuccine Alfredo

Ingredients:

- 350g fettuccine pasta
- 1 cup heavy cream
- 1/2 cup unsalted butter
- 1 cup freshly grated Parmesan cheese
- Salt and freshly ground black pepper, to taste
- Optional: chopped parsley for garnish

Instructions:

1. Bring a large pot of salted water to a boil. Cook the fettuccine according to package instructions until al dente. Reserve about 1 cup of pasta water before draining.
2. While the pasta is cooking, in a saucepan, heat the heavy cream and unsalted butter over medium heat. Stir occasionally until the butter is melted and the mixture is heated through but not boiling.
3. Once the pasta is cooked, drain it and return it to the pot. Pour the heated cream and butter mixture over the cooked fettuccine.
4. Add the freshly grated Parmesan cheese to the pot with the pasta and cream mixture. Toss everything together until the pasta is well coated and the cheese has melted, creating a creamy sauce. If the sauce is too thick, you can add a bit of the reserved pasta water to loosen it up.
5. Season the Fettuccine Alfredo with salt and freshly ground black pepper, to taste. Toss once more to combine.
6. Divide the Fettuccine Alfredo among serving plates. Garnish with chopped parsley, if desired. Serve immediately while hot.

Enjoy this decadent and creamy Fettuccine Alfredo as a comforting and satisfying meal!

Penne Arrabbiata

Ingredients:

- 350g penne pasta
- 2 tablespoons olive oil
- 4 cloves garlic, minced
- 1 teaspoon red pepper flakes (adjust to taste for desired spice level)
- 800g canned crushed tomatoes
- 1 teaspoon dried oregano
- Salt, to taste
- Freshly ground black pepper, to taste
- Fresh basil leaves, torn, for garnish (optional)
- Grated Parmesan cheese, for serving

Instructions:

1. Bring a large pot of salted water to a boil. Cook the penne pasta according to package instructions until al dente. Reserve about 1 cup of pasta water before draining.
2. While the pasta is cooking, heat the olive oil in a large skillet over medium heat. Add the minced garlic and red pepper flakes. Cook for 1-2 minutes until the garlic is fragrant and just beginning to brown.
3. Pour in the canned crushed tomatoes and dried oregano. Season with salt and freshly ground black pepper to taste. Stir to combine.
4. Allow the sauce to simmer for about 15-20 minutes, stirring occasionally, until it has thickened slightly and the flavors have melded together.
5. Once the sauce has reached your desired consistency, add the cooked penne pasta to the skillet with the arrabbiata sauce. Toss the pasta in the sauce until well coated. If the sauce is too thick, you can add a bit of the reserved pasta water to loosen it up.
6. Divide the Penne Arrabbiata among serving plates. Garnish with torn fresh basil leaves, if desired. Serve hot with grated Parmesan cheese on the side.

Enjoy the bold and spicy flavors of this delicious Penne Arrabbiata!

Linguine with Clam Sauce

Ingredients:

- 350g linguine pasta
- 2 tablespoons olive oil
- 4 cloves garlic, minced
- 1/2 teaspoon red pepper flakes (adjust to taste)
- 1/2 cup dry white wine
- 2 cans (about 400g each) chopped clams, drained, juice reserved
- 1/4 cup fresh parsley, chopped
- Salt, to taste
- Freshly ground black pepper, to taste
- Grated Parmesan cheese, for serving (optional)
- Additional chopped parsley, for garnish

Instructions:

1. Bring a large pot of salted water to a boil. Cook the linguine according to package instructions until al dente. Reserve about 1 cup of pasta water before draining.
2. While the pasta is cooking, heat the olive oil in a large skillet over medium heat. Add the minced garlic and red pepper flakes. Sauté for about 1 minute until the garlic is fragrant but not browned.
3. Pour in the dry white wine and bring it to a simmer. Allow it to cook for 2-3 minutes to reduce slightly.
4. Add the chopped clams to the skillet along with a portion of the reserved clam juice (start with about 1/2 cup). Stir to combine and simmer for another 2-3 minutes.
5. Once the linguine is cooked, add it directly to the skillet with the clam sauce. Toss the pasta in the sauce until well coated. If the sauce is too thick, you can add a bit of the reserved pasta water to loosen it up.
6. Season the Linguine with Clam Sauce with salt and freshly ground black pepper to taste. Stir in the chopped fresh parsley.
7. Divide the Linguine with Clam Sauce among serving plates. If desired, sprinkle with grated Parmesan cheese and additional chopped parsley for garnish.

Enjoy the delicious flavors of this Linguine with Clam Sauce, reminiscent of a seaside Italian trattoria!

Ravioli with Sage Butter Sauce

Ingredients:

- 350g ravioli (your choice of filling, such as cheese, spinach, or mushroom)
- 6 tablespoons unsalted butter
- 8-10 fresh sage leaves
- 2 cloves garlic, minced (optional)
- Salt, to taste
- Freshly ground black pepper, to taste
- Grated Parmesan cheese, for serving (optional)
- Chopped fresh parsley, for garnish (optional)

Instructions:

1. Bring a large pot of salted water to a boil. Cook the ravioli according to package instructions until they float to the surface and are tender, usually just a few minutes for fresh ravioli or a few minutes longer for frozen.
2. While the ravioli is cooking, prepare the sage butter sauce. In a large skillet, melt the unsalted butter over medium heat. Once the butter is melted and starts to foam, add the fresh sage leaves. Allow them to cook in the butter until they become crisp and fragrant, about 1-2 minutes. Be careful not to burn the butter.
3. If using minced garlic, add it to the skillet with the sage leaves and cook for an additional 1-2 minutes until fragrant.
4. Once the ravioli are cooked, use a slotted spoon to transfer them directly from the pot to the skillet with the sage butter sauce. Toss gently to coat the ravioli evenly in the sauce.
5. Season the Ravioli with Sage Butter Sauce with salt and freshly ground black pepper to taste.
6. Divide the ravioli among serving plates, making sure to spoon any remaining sage butter sauce over the top. If desired, sprinkle with grated Parmesan cheese and chopped fresh parsley for garnish.
7. Serve immediately while hot and enjoy the delicious flavors of this comforting dish!

Feel free to customize this recipe by using your favorite type of ravioli filling or adding additional ingredients such as toasted pine nuts or a squeeze of lemon juice for extra flavor.

Lasagna Bolognese

Ingredients:

For the Bolognese Sauce:

- 500g ground beef (or a mix of beef and pork)
- 1 onion, finely chopped
- 2 carrots, finely chopped
- 2 celery stalks, finely chopped
- 4 cloves garlic, minced
- 2 tablespoons tomato paste
- 800g canned crushed tomatoes
- 1 cup beef or chicken broth
- 1/2 cup dry red wine (optional)
- 1 teaspoon dried oregano
- 1 teaspoon dried basil
- Salt and freshly ground black pepper, to taste
- Olive oil, for cooking

For the Béchamel Sauce:

- 4 tablespoons unsalted butter
- 1/4 cup all-purpose flour
- 4 cups whole milk
- Salt and freshly ground black pepper, to taste
- Pinch of nutmeg

Other Ingredients:

- 350g lasagna noodles (oven-ready or cooked according to package instructions)
- 2 cups shredded mozzarella cheese
- 1 cup grated Parmesan cheese
- Fresh parsley, chopped, for garnish (optional)

Instructions:

1. To make the Bolognese sauce, heat a large skillet or Dutch oven over medium heat. Add a drizzle of olive oil and brown the ground beef, breaking it up with a spoon, until it's no longer pink. Remove the beef from the skillet and set aside.
2. In the same skillet, add a bit more olive oil if needed and sauté the onion, carrots, and celery until softened, about 5-7 minutes. Add the minced garlic and cook for an additional minute.
3. Stir in the tomato paste and cook for 1-2 minutes to caramelize it slightly. Then, return the cooked ground beef to the skillet.
4. Pour in the crushed tomatoes, beef or chicken broth, and red wine (if using). Add the dried oregano and basil. Season with salt and freshly ground black pepper to taste. Stir to combine.
5. Bring the mixture to a simmer, then reduce the heat to low and let it simmer gently for about 1-2 hours, stirring occasionally, until the sauce has thickened and the flavors have melded together. If the sauce gets too thick, you can add a bit of water or broth to adjust the consistency.
6. Meanwhile, prepare the béchamel sauce. In a medium saucepan, melt the butter over medium heat. Once melted, whisk in the flour to form a roux. Cook the roux for 1-2 minutes until it's golden in color and fragrant.
7. Gradually whisk in the milk, a little at a time, until smooth and well combined. Cook the sauce, stirring constantly, until it thickens enough to coat the back of a spoon, about 5-7 minutes.
8. Season the béchamel sauce with salt, freshly ground black pepper, and a pinch of nutmeg. Remove the saucepan from the heat and set aside.
9. Preheat your oven to 375°F (190°C). Lightly grease a 9x13-inch baking dish with olive oil or cooking spray.
10. To assemble the lasagna, spread a thin layer of the Bolognese sauce on the bottom of the prepared baking dish. Arrange a layer of lasagna noodles on top, slightly overlapping them.
11. Spread a layer of the Bolognese sauce over the noodles, followed by a layer of the béchamel sauce, and a sprinkle of mozzarella and Parmesan cheese. Repeat the layers until all ingredients are used up, ending with a layer of cheese on top.
12. Cover the baking dish with aluminum foil and bake in the preheated oven for 30 minutes. Then, remove the foil and continue baking for an additional 15-20 minutes, or until the cheese is golden and bubbly.
13. Once baked, remove the lasagna from the oven and let it cool for a few minutes before slicing. Garnish with chopped fresh parsley, if desired.
14. Serve the Lasagna Bolognese hot, and enjoy the hearty and comforting flavors!

Feel free to customize this recipe by adding additional ingredients such as sautéed mushrooms or spinach to the layers, or by using your favorite cheese blend.

Tagliatelle with Pesto Genovese

Ingredients:

For the Pesto Genovese:

- 2 cups fresh basil leaves, packed
- 1/2 cup grated Parmesan cheese
- 1/4 cup pine nuts (or walnuts)
- 2 garlic cloves, peeled
- 1/2 cup extra virgin olive oil
- Salt and freshly ground black pepper, to taste

For the Tagliatelle:

- 350g tagliatelle pasta
- Salt, for pasta water
- Grated Parmesan cheese, for serving (optional)
- Extra basil leaves, for garnish (optional)

Instructions:

1. Prepare the Pesto Genovese: In a food processor or blender, combine the fresh basil leaves, grated Parmesan cheese, pine nuts (or walnuts), and garlic cloves. Pulse several times until the ingredients are finely chopped and well combined.
2. With the food processor running, gradually drizzle in the extra virgin olive oil until the pesto reaches a smooth and creamy consistency. If the pesto is too thick, you can add a bit more olive oil to thin it out. Season with salt and freshly ground black pepper to taste. Set the pesto aside.
3. Cook the tagliatelle pasta in a large pot of salted boiling water according to package instructions until al dente. Reserve about 1 cup of pasta water before draining.
4. Once the pasta is cooked, drain it and transfer it to a large serving bowl. Add a few spoonfuls of the prepared Pesto Genovese to the pasta and toss gently to

coat. If the pesto is too thick, you can add a bit of the reserved pasta water to loosen it up and help it adhere to the pasta.
5. Divide the Tagliatelle with Pesto Genovese among serving plates. If desired, sprinkle with additional grated Parmesan cheese and garnish with extra basil leaves.
6. Serve the Tagliatelle with Pesto Genovese immediately, and enjoy the fresh and aromatic flavors!

Feel free to adjust the quantities of the ingredients in the pesto sauce to suit your taste preferences. You can also add a squeeze of fresh lemon juice for a hint of brightness, or incorporate other ingredients such as cherry tomatoes or grilled chicken for additional flavor and texture.

Gnocchi alla Sorrentina

Ingredients:

- 500g potato gnocchi (store-bought or homemade)
- 2 tablespoons olive oil
- 2 cloves garlic, minced
- 800g canned crushed tomatoes
- 1 teaspoon dried oregano
- Salt and freshly ground black pepper, to taste
- 200g fresh mozzarella cheese, sliced
- Fresh basil leaves, torn, for garnish
- Grated Parmesan cheese, for serving (optional)

Instructions:

1. Preheat your oven to 375°F (190°C). Grease a baking dish with olive oil or cooking spray.
2. Bring a large pot of salted water to a boil. Cook the potato gnocchi according to package instructions until they float to the surface, usually just a few minutes for fresh gnocchi or a few minutes longer for frozen. Drain the gnocchi and set aside.
3. While the gnocchi is cooking, prepare the tomato sauce. In a large skillet, heat the olive oil over medium heat. Add the minced garlic and sauté for 1-2 minutes until fragrant.
4. Pour in the canned crushed tomatoes and add the dried oregano. Season with salt and freshly ground black pepper to taste. Stir to combine and let the sauce simmer for about 10-15 minutes, allowing the flavors to meld together and the sauce to thicken slightly.
5. Once the sauce is ready, add the cooked gnocchi to the skillet with the tomato sauce. Toss gently to coat the gnocchi evenly in the sauce.
6. Transfer the sauced gnocchi to the prepared baking dish. Arrange the sliced fresh mozzarella evenly on top of the gnocchi.
7. Bake the Gnocchi alla Sorrentina in the preheated oven for 15-20 minutes, or until the mozzarella is melted and bubbly and the edges are golden brown.
8. Once baked, remove the baking dish from the oven and garnish the Gnocchi alla Sorrentina with torn fresh basil leaves.
9. Serve the Gnocchi alla Sorrentina hot, with grated Parmesan cheese on the side for sprinkling, if desired.

Enjoy the comforting and cheesy goodness of this classic Italian dish!

Farfalle with Creamy Mushroom Sauce

Ingredients:

- 350g farfalle (bowtie) pasta
- 2 tablespoons olive oil
- 500g mushrooms (such as cremini or button), sliced
- 4 cloves garlic, minced
- 1 small onion, finely chopped
- 1 cup heavy cream
- 1/2 cup chicken or vegetable broth
- 1/4 cup grated Parmesan cheese
- 2 tablespoons chopped fresh parsley
- Salt and freshly ground black pepper, to taste
- Pinch of red pepper flakes (optional)
- Grated Parmesan cheese, for serving

Instructions:

1. Cook the farfalle pasta in a large pot of salted boiling water according to package instructions until al dente. Drain the pasta and set aside, reserving about 1 cup of pasta water.
2. In a large skillet, heat the olive oil over medium heat. Add the sliced mushrooms and cook, stirring occasionally, until they are golden brown and softened, about 5-7 minutes.
3. Add the minced garlic and chopped onion to the skillet with the mushrooms. Sauté for another 2-3 minutes until the garlic is fragrant and the onion is translucent.
4. Pour in the heavy cream and chicken or vegetable broth. Bring the mixture to a simmer and let it cook for 5-7 minutes, allowing the sauce to thicken slightly.
5. Stir in the grated Parmesan cheese and chopped fresh parsley. Season the sauce with salt, freshly ground black pepper, and a pinch of red pepper flakes, if desired. Taste and adjust seasoning as needed.
6. Add the cooked farfalle pasta to the skillet with the creamy mushroom sauce. Toss everything together until the pasta is evenly coated in the sauce. If the sauce is too thick, you can add a bit of the reserved pasta water to loosen it up.

7. Once everything is heated through and well combined, remove the skillet from the heat.
8. Divide the farfalle with creamy mushroom sauce among serving plates. Serve hot, with additional grated Parmesan cheese on top for sprinkling.

Enjoy this delicious and comforting farfalle pasta dish with creamy mushroom sauce!

Cannelloni Ricotta e Spinaci

Ingredients:

For the Filling:

- 250g fresh spinach, washed and chopped
- 400g ricotta cheese
- 1 cup grated Parmesan cheese
- 2 cloves garlic, minced
- Salt and freshly ground black pepper, to taste
- Pinch of nutmeg (optional)

For the Tomato Sauce:

- 800g canned crushed tomatoes
- 2 tablespoons olive oil
- 1 onion, finely chopped
- 2 cloves garlic, minced
- 1 teaspoon dried oregano
- Salt and freshly ground black pepper, to taste

Other Ingredients:

- 250g cannelloni tubes (about 12 tubes)
- 1 cup shredded mozzarella cheese
- Fresh basil leaves, torn, for garnish (optional)

Instructions:

1. Preheat your oven to 375°F (190°C). Grease a large baking dish with olive oil or cooking spray.
2. Prepare the filling: In a large skillet, heat a drizzle of olive oil over medium heat. Add the minced garlic and chopped spinach. Cook, stirring occasionally, until the

spinach wilts and any excess moisture evaporates, about 5-7 minutes. Remove from heat and let cool slightly.
3. In a mixing bowl, combine the cooked spinach, ricotta cheese, grated Parmesan cheese, minced garlic, salt, freshly ground black pepper, and a pinch of nutmeg (if using). Mix well to combine.
4. Prepare the tomato sauce: In a separate skillet, heat the olive oil over medium heat. Add the chopped onion and minced garlic. Sauté until softened and fragrant, about 5 minutes.
5. Pour in the canned crushed tomatoes and add the dried oregano. Season with salt and freshly ground black pepper to taste. Let the sauce simmer for 10-15 minutes, allowing the flavors to meld together.
6. While the sauce is simmering, prepare the cannelloni tubes according to package instructions. Some cannelloni tubes may require pre-cooking, while others can be filled raw.
7. Once the cannelloni tubes are cooked or softened, carefully fill each tube with the ricotta and spinach mixture using a spoon or piping bag.
8. Spread a thin layer of the tomato sauce on the bottom of the prepared baking dish. Arrange the filled cannelloni tubes in a single layer on top of the sauce.
9. Pour the remaining tomato sauce over the cannelloni tubes, covering them completely. Sprinkle shredded mozzarella cheese evenly over the top.
10. Cover the baking dish with aluminum foil and bake in the preheated oven for 25-30 minutes, or until the cannelloni are tender and the cheese is melted and bubbly.
11. Once baked, remove the foil and let the Cannelloni Ricotta e Spinaci cool for a few minutes before serving.
12. Garnish with torn fresh basil leaves, if desired, and serve hot.

Enjoy the delicious flavors of this Cannelloni Ricotta e Spinaci with your favorite side salad or crusty bread!

Orecchiette with Broccoli Rabe and Sausage

Ingredients:

- 350g orecchiette pasta
- 1 bunch broccoli rabe (rapini), washed and trimmed
- 250g Italian sausage, casings removed
- 3 cloves garlic, minced
- 1/4 teaspoon red pepper flakes (adjust to taste)
- 1/4 cup extra virgin olive oil
- Salt, to taste
- Grated Parmesan cheese, for serving (optional)

Instructions:

1. Bring a large pot of salted water to a boil. Add the orecchiette pasta and cook according to package instructions until al dente. Drain the pasta, reserving about 1 cup of pasta water.
2. While the pasta is cooking, blanch the broccoli rabe in a pot of boiling salted water for about 2 minutes. Drain and rinse under cold water to stop the cooking process. Chop the broccoli rabe into bite-sized pieces and set aside.
3. In a large skillet, heat the olive oil over medium heat. Add the Italian sausage, breaking it up with a spoon, and cook until browned and cooked through, about 5-7 minutes.
4. Add the minced garlic and red pepper flakes to the skillet with the sausage. Sauté for 1-2 minutes until the garlic is fragrant.
5. Add the chopped broccoli rabe to the skillet with the sausage. Sauté for another 3-4 minutes, stirring occasionally, until the broccoli rabe is tender.
6. Toss the cooked orecchiette pasta into the skillet with the sausage and broccoli rabe. If the mixture seems dry, add some of the reserved pasta water to loosen it up.
7. Season the Orecchiette with Broccoli Rabe and Sausage with salt to taste. Stir everything together until the pasta is well coated in the sausage and broccoli rabe mixture.
8. Divide the Orecchiette with Broccoli Rabe and Sausage among serving plates. Serve hot, with grated Parmesan cheese on top for sprinkling, if desired.

Enjoy the delicious flavors of this hearty and satisfying Italian pasta dish!

Tortellini in Brodo (Tortellini in Broth)

Ingredients:

For the Tortellini:

- 350g fresh or dried tortellini (cheese, meat, or your preferred filling)
- Salt, for seasoning water (optional)

For the Broth:

- 2 liters (8 cups) chicken broth or vegetable broth
- 2 cloves garlic, minced
- 1 small onion, finely chopped
- 2 carrots, diced
- 2 celery stalks, diced
- 1 tablespoon olive oil
- Salt and freshly ground black pepper, to taste
- Fresh parsley, chopped, for garnish (optional)
- Grated Parmesan cheese, for serving (optional)

Instructions:

1. In a large pot, heat the olive oil over medium heat. Add the minced garlic, chopped onion, diced carrots, and diced celery. Sauté for 5-7 minutes until the vegetables are softened and aromatic.
2. Pour in the chicken broth or vegetable broth, and bring the mixture to a simmer. Let it simmer gently for about 15-20 minutes to allow the flavors to meld together.
3. While the broth is simmering, bring a separate pot of water to a boil. If using dried tortellini, cook them according to package instructions until al dente. If using fresh tortellini, they usually only need a few minutes to cook, so adjust accordingly. Add salt to the boiling water if desired.
4. Once the tortellini are cooked, drain them and set aside.
5. Season the broth with salt and freshly ground black pepper to taste, adjusting as needed.

6. To serve, divide the cooked tortellini among serving bowls. Ladle the hot broth over the tortellini, making sure to include some of the vegetables in each bowl.
7. Garnish the Tortellini in Brodo with chopped fresh parsley and grated Parmesan cheese, if desired.
8. Serve immediately, accompanied by crusty bread or a side salad if desired.

Enjoy the comforting and nourishing flavors of this classic Italian dish!

Spaghetti alla Puttanesca

Ingredients:

- 350g spaghetti
- 4 tablespoons olive oil
- 4 cloves garlic, minced
- 4-6 anchovy fillets, chopped (optional)
- 1 teaspoon red pepper flakes (adjust to taste)
- 400g canned diced tomatoes
- 1/2 cup pitted Kalamata olives, chopped
- 2 tablespoons capers, drained
- Salt, to taste
- Freshly ground black pepper, to taste
- Chopped fresh parsley, for garnish
- Grated Parmesan cheese, for serving (optional)

Instructions:

1. Bring a large pot of salted water to a boil. Cook the spaghetti according to package instructions until al dente. Reserve about 1 cup of pasta water before draining.
2. While the pasta is cooking, heat the olive oil in a large skillet over medium heat. Add the minced garlic and chopped anchovy fillets (if using). Cook for 1-2 minutes until the garlic is fragrant and the anchovies have melted into the oil.
3. Add the red pepper flakes to the skillet and cook for another 1-2 minutes.
4. Pour in the canned diced tomatoes along with their juices. Stir to combine.
5. Add the chopped Kalamata olives and drained capers to the skillet. Stir well to incorporate all the ingredients.
6. Let the sauce simmer for about 10-15 minutes, stirring occasionally, until it has thickened slightly and the flavors have melded together. If the sauce is too thick, you can add a bit of the reserved pasta water to thin it out.
7. Once the sauce has reached your desired consistency, season it with salt and freshly ground black pepper to taste.
8. Add the cooked spaghetti to the skillet with the puttanesca sauce. Toss everything together until the pasta is well coated in the sauce.

9. Divide the Spaghetti alla Puttanesca among serving plates. Garnish with chopped fresh parsley and grated Parmesan cheese, if desired.
10. Serve immediately, and enjoy the bold and savory flavors of this classic Italian pasta dish!

Feel free to adjust the quantities of the ingredients or customize the recipe to suit your taste preferences. You can also add extra ingredients like anchovies or chopped tomatoes for added depth of flavor.

Rigatoni alla Norma

Ingredients:

- 350g rigatoni pasta
- 1 large eggplant, diced into small cubes
- Salt, for eggplant
- Olive oil, for frying
- 2 tablespoons olive oil
- 4 cloves garlic, minced
- 400g canned diced tomatoes
- 1 teaspoon dried oregano
- 1/2 teaspoon red pepper flakes (adjust to taste)
- Salt and freshly ground black pepper, to taste
- Fresh basil leaves, torn, for garnish
- Grated ricotta salata cheese, for serving

Instructions:

1. Place the diced eggplant in a colander and sprinkle generously with salt. Let it sit for about 30 minutes to release excess moisture. Rinse the eggplant cubes under cold water and pat them dry with paper towels.
2. Heat a generous amount of olive oil in a large skillet over medium-high heat. Fry the eggplant cubes in batches until golden brown and tender. Remove them from the skillet and drain them on paper towels to remove excess oil. Set aside.
3. In the same skillet, heat 2 tablespoons of olive oil over medium heat. Add the minced garlic and sauté for 1-2 minutes until fragrant.
4. Pour in the canned diced tomatoes along with their juices. Add the dried oregano and red pepper flakes. Season with salt and freshly ground black pepper to taste. Stir to combine.
5. Let the tomato sauce simmer for about 10-15 minutes, stirring occasionally, until it has thickened slightly and the flavors have melded together.
6. While the sauce is simmering, bring a large pot of salted water to a boil. Cook the rigatoni pasta according to package instructions until al dente. Drain the pasta, reserving about 1 cup of pasta water.
7. Add the fried eggplant cubes to the skillet with the tomato sauce. Stir to incorporate.

8. Add the cooked rigatoni pasta to the skillet with the sauce and eggplant. Toss everything together until the pasta is well coated in the sauce.
9. If the sauce is too thick, you can add a bit of the reserved pasta water to thin it out and help it adhere to the pasta.
10. Divide the Rigatoni alla Norma among serving plates. Garnish with torn fresh basil leaves and grated ricotta salata cheese.
11. Serve immediately, and enjoy the delicious flavors of this classic Sicilian pasta dish!

Feel free to adjust the quantities of the ingredients or customize the recipe to suit your taste preferences.

Pappardelle with Wild Boar Ragu

Ingredients:

For the Wild Boar Ragu:

- 500g wild boar meat, diced (substitute with pork shoulder if wild boar is not available)
- 2 tablespoons olive oil
- 1 onion, finely chopped
- 2 carrots, finely chopped
- 2 celery stalks, finely chopped
- 4 cloves garlic, minced
- 200ml red wine
- 800g canned crushed tomatoes
- 2 tablespoons tomato paste
- 2 bay leaves
- 1 teaspoon dried thyme
- Salt and freshly ground black pepper, to taste

For the Pappardelle:

- 350g pappardelle pasta
- Salt, for boiling water

Instructions:

1. Heat the olive oil in a large Dutch oven or heavy-bottomed pot over medium heat. Add the diced wild boar meat and cook until browned on all sides. Remove the browned meat from the pot and set aside.
2. In the same pot, add the chopped onion, carrots, and celery. Cook, stirring occasionally, until the vegetables are softened, about 5-7 minutes.
3. Add the minced garlic to the pot and cook for another 1-2 minutes until fragrant.
4. Deglaze the pot with red wine, scraping up any browned bits from the bottom with a wooden spoon.

5. Return the browned wild boar meat to the pot. Add the crushed tomatoes, tomato paste, bay leaves, and dried thyme. Season with salt and freshly ground black pepper to taste.
6. Bring the mixture to a simmer, then reduce the heat to low. Cover and let the ragu sauce simmer gently for about 2-3 hours, stirring occasionally, until the meat is tender and the flavors have melded together. If the sauce becomes too thick, you can add a bit of water or broth to reach your desired consistency.
7. While the ragu is simmering, bring a large pot of salted water to a boil. Cook the pappardelle pasta according to package instructions until al dente. Drain the pasta, reserving about 1 cup of pasta water.
8. Add the cooked pappardelle pasta to the pot with the wild boar ragu sauce. Toss gently to coat the pasta evenly in the sauce. If the sauce is too thick, you can add a bit of the reserved pasta water to loosen it up.
9. Divide the Pappardelle with Wild Boar Ragu among serving plates. Serve hot, garnished with freshly grated Parmesan cheese and chopped fresh parsley, if desired.

Enjoy the rich and comforting flavors of this delicious Italian pasta dish!

Conchiglie with Tomato and Basil Sauce

Ingredients:

- 350g conchiglie (shell) pasta
- 3 tablespoons olive oil
- 4 cloves garlic, minced
- 800g canned crushed tomatoes
- 1 teaspoon dried oregano
- Salt and freshly ground black pepper, to taste
- 1/4 teaspoon red pepper flakes (optional)
- 1/4 cup chopped fresh basil leaves
- Grated Parmesan cheese, for serving (optional)

Instructions:

1. Bring a large pot of salted water to a boil. Cook the conchiglie pasta according to package instructions until al dente. Drain the pasta and set aside.
2. While the pasta is cooking, heat the olive oil in a large skillet over medium heat. Add the minced garlic and sauté for 1-2 minutes until fragrant.
3. Pour in the canned crushed tomatoes and add the dried oregano. Season with salt, freshly ground black pepper, and red pepper flakes (if using). Stir to combine.
4. Let the tomato sauce simmer for about 10-15 minutes, stirring occasionally, until it has thickened slightly and the flavors have melded together.
5. Once the sauce is ready, add the cooked conchiglie pasta to the skillet. Toss gently to coat the pasta evenly in the sauce.
6. Remove the skillet from the heat and stir in the chopped fresh basil leaves.
7. Divide the Conchiglie with Tomato and Basil Sauce among serving plates. Serve hot, with grated Parmesan cheese on top for sprinkling, if desired.
8. Enjoy the simple and delicious flavors of this classic Italian pasta dish!

Feel free to customize the recipe by adding extra ingredients such as sautéed vegetables, cooked shrimp, or grilled chicken for added flavor and protein. You can also adjust the seasoning according to your taste preferences.

Paccheri with Seafood

Ingredients:

- 350g paccheri pasta
- 250g shrimp, peeled and deveined
- 250g clams, scrubbed
- 250g mussels, cleaned and debearded
- 200g calamari rings
- 4 cloves garlic, minced
- 1 small onion, finely chopped
- 2 tablespoons olive oil
- 400g canned crushed tomatoes
- 1/2 cup white wine
- 1 teaspoon dried oregano
- 1/2 teaspoon red pepper flakes (adjust to taste)
- Salt and freshly ground black pepper, to taste
- Fresh parsley, chopped, for garnish
- Grated Parmesan cheese, for serving (optional)
- Lemon wedges, for serving (optional)

Instructions:

1. Bring a large pot of salted water to a boil. Cook the paccheri pasta according to package instructions until al dente. Drain the pasta and set aside.
2. While the pasta is cooking, heat the olive oil in a large skillet over medium heat. Add the minced garlic and chopped onion. Sauté until the onion is softened and translucent, about 5 minutes.
3. Add the cleaned shrimp, clams, mussels, and calamari rings to the skillet. Cook, stirring occasionally, until the seafood is partially cooked, about 3-4 minutes.
4. Pour in the white wine and let it simmer for a couple of minutes to cook off the alcohol.
5. Stir in the canned crushed tomatoes, dried oregano, and red pepper flakes. Season with salt and freshly ground black pepper to taste.
6. Let the sauce simmer for about 5-7 minutes, or until the seafood is fully cooked and the flavors have melded together. Discard any clams or mussels that do not open.

7. Add the cooked paccheri pasta to the skillet with the seafood sauce. Toss gently to coat the pasta evenly in the sauce.
8. Divide the Paccheri with Seafood among serving plates. Garnish with chopped fresh parsley.
9. Serve hot, with grated Parmesan cheese and lemon wedges on the side for squeezing over the pasta, if desired.
10. Enjoy the delicious flavors of this seafood-packed pasta dish!

Feel free to adjust the types of seafood used according to your preferences or what's available. You can also add extra ingredients such as cherry tomatoes or chopped bell peppers for added flavor and color.

Cacio e Pepe

Ingredients:

- 350g spaghetti or other long pasta
- 1 cup finely grated Pecorino Romano cheese
- 2 teaspoons freshly ground black pepper
- Salt, for pasta water

Instructions:

1. Bring a large pot of salted water to a boil. Add the spaghetti and cook according to package instructions until al dente.
2. While the pasta is cooking, combine the grated Pecorino Romano cheese and freshly ground black pepper in a large mixing bowl.
3. Once the pasta is cooked, reserve about 1 cup of pasta water, then drain the pasta.
4. Immediately add the hot drained pasta to the bowl with the cheese and pepper mixture.
5. Quickly toss the pasta with the cheese and pepper, adding a few tablespoons of the reserved pasta water at a time until a creamy sauce forms and coats the pasta evenly. The heat from the pasta will melt the cheese and create a creamy sauce.
6. Continue tossing the pasta until the cheese has melted and the sauce is smooth and creamy. Adjust the consistency with more pasta water if needed.
7. Serve the Cacio e Pepe immediately, garnished with additional freshly ground black pepper and grated Pecorino Romano cheese, if desired.
8. Enjoy this simple yet delicious pasta dish that celebrates the flavors of Pecorino Romano cheese and black pepper!

Cacio e Pepe is best enjoyed right after it's made, so be sure to serve it immediately while it's hot and creamy.

Bucatini all'Amatriciana

Ingredients:

- 350g bucatini pasta
- 150g guanciale, diced (substitute with pancetta or bacon if guanciale is not available)
- 1 tablespoon olive oil
- 1 small onion, finely chopped
- 2 cloves garlic, minced
- 400g canned crushed tomatoes
- 1/2 teaspoon red pepper flakes (adjust to taste)
- Salt, to taste
- Freshly ground black pepper, to taste
- Grated Pecorino Romano cheese, for serving
- Chopped fresh parsley, for garnish (optional)

Instructions:

1. Bring a large pot of salted water to a boil. Cook the bucatini pasta according to package instructions until al dente. Reserve about 1 cup of pasta water, then drain the pasta and set aside.
2. In a large skillet, heat the olive oil over medium heat. Add the diced guanciale and cook until crispy and golden brown, about 5-7 minutes.
3. Add the chopped onion to the skillet with the crispy guanciale. Cook, stirring occasionally, until the onion is softened and translucent, about 5 minutes.
4. Add the minced garlic to the skillet and cook for another 1-2 minutes until fragrant.
5. Pour in the canned crushed tomatoes and add the red pepper flakes. Season with salt and freshly ground black pepper to taste. Stir to combine.
6. Let the sauce simmer for about 10-15 minutes, stirring occasionally, until it has thickened slightly and the flavors have melded together.
7. Once the sauce is ready, add the cooked bucatini pasta to the skillet. Toss everything together until the pasta is well coated in the sauce.
8. If the sauce is too thick, you can add a bit of the reserved pasta water to loosen it up and help it adhere to the pasta.

9. Divide the Bucatini all'Amatriciana among serving plates. Serve hot, garnished with grated Pecorino Romano cheese and chopped fresh parsley, if desired.
10. Enjoy the bold and savory flavors of this classic Italian pasta dish!

Feel free to adjust the quantities of the ingredients or customize the recipe to suit your taste preferences. You can also add extra red pepper flakes for a spicier kick, or garnish with additional grated cheese for added richness.

Aglio e Olio (Garlic and Olive Oil Pasta)

Ingredients:

- 350g spaghetti or linguine pasta
- 1/3 cup extra virgin olive oil
- 6 cloves garlic, thinly sliced
- 1 teaspoon red pepper flakes (adjust to taste)
- Salt, to taste
- Freshly ground black pepper, to taste
- Chopped fresh parsley, for garnish
- Grated Parmesan cheese, for serving (optional)
- Lemon zest, for serving (optional)

Instructions:

1. Bring a large pot of salted water to a boil. Cook the spaghetti or linguine pasta according to package instructions until al dente. Reserve about 1 cup of pasta water, then drain the pasta and set aside.
2. While the pasta is cooking, heat the olive oil in a large skillet over medium heat. Add the thinly sliced garlic and red pepper flakes. Cook, stirring frequently, until the garlic is golden brown and fragrant, about 2-3 minutes. Be careful not to burn the garlic.
3. Once the garlic is golden brown, remove the skillet from the heat. If the garlic starts to brown too quickly, you can remove the skillet from the heat to prevent it from burning.
4. Add the cooked pasta to the skillet with the garlic and olive oil. Toss everything together until the pasta is well coated in the oil and garlic mixture.
5. If the pasta seems too dry, you can add a bit of the reserved pasta water to loosen it up and help the sauce adhere to the pasta.
6. Season the Aglio e Olio with salt and freshly ground black pepper to taste. Toss once more to combine.
7. Divide the pasta among serving plates. Garnish with chopped fresh parsley.
8. Serve hot, with grated Parmesan cheese and lemon zest on the side for sprinkling over the pasta, if desired.
9. Enjoy the simple and delicious flavors of this classic Italian pasta dish!

Aglio e Olio is best enjoyed immediately while it's hot and freshly made. It's perfect for a quick weeknight dinner or whenever you're craving a satisfying and flavorful pasta dish.

Strozzapreti with Pancetta and Peas

Ingredients:

- 350g strozzapreti pasta (substitute with penne or fusilli if strozzapreti is not available)
- 150g pancetta, diced
- 1 tablespoon olive oil
- 1 small onion, finely chopped
- 2 cloves garlic, minced
- 1 cup frozen peas, thawed
- 1 cup heavy cream
- 1/2 cup grated Parmesan cheese
- Salt and freshly ground black pepper, to taste
- Chopped fresh parsley, for garnish (optional)

Instructions:

1. Bring a large pot of salted water to a boil. Cook the strozzapreti pasta according to package instructions until al dente. Drain the pasta and set aside.
2. While the pasta is cooking, heat the olive oil in a large skillet over medium heat. Add the diced pancetta and cook until crispy and golden brown, about 5-7 minutes.
3. Add the chopped onion to the skillet with the crispy pancetta. Cook, stirring occasionally, until the onion is softened and translucent, about 5 minutes.
4. Add the minced garlic to the skillet and cook for another 1-2 minutes until fragrant.
5. Stir in the thawed peas and cook for 2-3 minutes until heated through.
6. Pour in the heavy cream and bring the mixture to a simmer. Let it simmer gently for about 3-5 minutes to thicken slightly.
7. Stir in the grated Parmesan cheese until melted and smooth. Season the sauce with salt and freshly ground black pepper to taste.
8. Add the cooked strozzapreti pasta to the skillet with the creamy pancetta and pea sauce. Toss everything together until the pasta is well coated in the sauce.
9. Divide the Strozzapreti with Pancetta and Peas among serving plates. Garnish with chopped fresh parsley, if desired.

10. Serve hot, and enjoy the creamy and savory flavors of this delicious Italian pasta dish!

Feel free to adjust the quantities of the ingredients or customize the recipe to suit your taste preferences. You can also add extra ingredients such as cherry tomatoes or chopped spinach for added flavor and color.

Cavatelli with Broccoli and Sausage

Ingredients:

- 350g cavatelli pasta
- 2 tablespoons olive oil
- 250g Italian sausage, casings removed
- 3 cloves garlic, minced
- 1 small onion, finely chopped
- 1 head broccoli, cut into small florets
- 1/2 cup chicken or vegetable broth
- Salt and freshly ground black pepper, to taste
- Grated Parmesan cheese, for serving
- Red pepper flakes, for serving (optional)

Instructions:

1. Bring a large pot of salted water to a boil. Cook the cavatelli pasta according to package instructions until al dente. Drain the pasta and set aside.
2. While the pasta is cooking, heat the olive oil in a large skillet over medium heat. Add the Italian sausage, breaking it up with a spoon, and cook until browned and cooked through, about 5-7 minutes.
3. Add the minced garlic and chopped onion to the skillet with the sausage. Sauté for another 2-3 minutes until the garlic is fragrant and the onion is translucent.
4. Add the broccoli florets to the skillet with the sausage mixture. Pour in the chicken or vegetable broth. Cover the skillet and let the broccoli steam for about 5 minutes until tender.
5. Once the broccoli is tender, remove the lid from the skillet and let any excess liquid evaporate.
6. Add the cooked cavatelli pasta to the skillet with the sausage and broccoli. Toss everything together until the pasta is well coated in the sausage and broccoli mixture.
7. Season the Cavatelli with Broccoli and Sausage with salt and freshly ground black pepper to taste.
8. Divide the pasta among serving plates. Serve hot, garnished with grated Parmesan cheese and red pepper flakes, if desired.
9. Enjoy the delicious flavors of this hearty and satisfying Italian pasta dish!

Feel free to adjust the quantities of the ingredients or customize the recipe to suit your taste preferences. You can also add extra ingredients such as sun-dried tomatoes or mushrooms for added flavor and texture.

Manicotti alla Fiorentina

Ingredients:

For the Manicotti:

- 14 manicotti pasta tubes
- 500g ricotta cheese
- 300g frozen spinach, thawed and drained
- 1 cup grated Parmesan cheese
- 2 eggs
- 1 teaspoon garlic powder
- Salt and pepper to taste
- Pinch of nutmeg
- Fresh parsley, chopped, for garnish (optional)

For the Tomato Sauce:

- 800g canned crushed tomatoes
- 2 cloves garlic, minced
- 2 tablespoons olive oil
- 1 teaspoon dried oregano
- Salt and pepper to taste

For the Béchamel Sauce:

- 4 tablespoons butter
- 4 tablespoons all-purpose flour
- 2 cups milk
- Salt, pepper, and nutmeg to taste

Instructions:

1. Preheat your oven to 375°F (190°C). Grease a large baking dish with butter or olive oil.

2. Cook the manicotti pasta tubes according to package instructions until they are al dente. Drain and set aside.
3. In a mixing bowl, combine the ricotta cheese, grated Parmesan cheese, thawed and drained spinach, eggs, garlic powder, salt, pepper, and nutmeg. Mix until well combined.
4. Fill each cooked manicotti tube with the spinach and ricotta mixture using a spoon or a piping bag. Place the filled manicotti tubes in the prepared baking dish.
5. To make the tomato sauce, heat the olive oil in a saucepan over medium heat. Add the minced garlic and cook until fragrant, about 1 minute. Pour in the crushed tomatoes and add the dried oregano, salt, and pepper. Let the sauce simmer for 10-15 minutes, stirring occasionally.
6. To make the béchamel sauce, melt the butter in a saucepan over medium heat. Add the flour and cook, stirring constantly, for 1-2 minutes to make a roux. Gradually whisk in the milk until smooth. Cook the sauce, stirring constantly, until it thickens and coats the back of a spoon. Season with salt, pepper, and a pinch of nutmeg.
7. Pour the tomato sauce over the filled manicotti in the baking dish, covering them evenly. Then pour the béchamel sauce over the tomato sauce.
8. Cover the baking dish with aluminum foil and bake in the preheated oven for 25-30 minutes, or until the sauce is bubbly and the manicotti are heated through.
9. Once baked, remove the foil and let the manicotti rest for a few minutes before serving.
10. Garnish with chopped fresh parsley, if desired, and serve hot.

Enjoy the rich and comforting flavors of Manicotti alla Fiorentina!

Fusilli with Roasted Vegetables

Ingredients:

- 350g fusilli pasta
- 2 bell peppers (red, yellow, or orange), sliced
- 1 zucchini, sliced into rounds
- 1 yellow squash, sliced into rounds
- 1 red onion, sliced
- 1 cup cherry tomatoes
- 3 cloves garlic, minced
- 3 tablespoons olive oil
- 1 teaspoon dried Italian herbs (such as basil, oregano, and thyme)
- Salt and freshly ground black pepper, to taste
- Grated Parmesan cheese, for serving (optional)
- Fresh basil leaves, torn, for garnish (optional)

Instructions:

1. Preheat your oven to 400°F (200°C). Line a baking sheet with parchment paper or aluminum foil for easy cleanup.
2. In a large mixing bowl, combine the sliced bell peppers, zucchini, yellow squash, red onion, cherry tomatoes, minced garlic, olive oil, dried Italian herbs, salt, and pepper. Toss everything together until the vegetables are evenly coated with the oil and seasonings.
3. Spread the seasoned vegetables in a single layer on the prepared baking sheet. Roast in the preheated oven for 20-25 minutes, or until the vegetables are tender and slightly caramelized, stirring halfway through.
4. While the vegetables are roasting, cook the fusilli pasta according to package instructions until al dente. Drain the pasta and set aside.
5. Once the vegetables are done roasting, remove them from the oven and transfer them to a large mixing bowl. Add the cooked fusilli pasta to the bowl with the roasted vegetables.
6. Toss the fusilli pasta and roasted vegetables together until they are well combined.
7. Serve the Fusilli with Roasted Vegetables hot, garnished with grated Parmesan cheese and torn fresh basil leaves, if desired.

8. Enjoy this flavorful and colorful pasta dish as a satisfying main course or side dish!

Feel free to customize the recipe by adding other vegetables of your choice, such as eggplant, mushrooms, or asparagus. You can also drizzle a little balsamic glaze over the finished dish for extra flavor.

Pici with Tuscan Sausage Sauce

Ingredients:

For the Pici Pasta:

- 350g all-purpose flour
- 150ml warm water
- 1 tablespoon olive oil
- Pinch of salt

For the Tuscan Sausage Sauce:

- 250g Tuscan sausage (or any mild Italian sausage), casings removed
- 2 tablespoons olive oil
- 1 onion, finely chopped
- 2 cloves garlic, minced
- 1/2 cup dry white wine
- 400g canned crushed tomatoes
- 1 teaspoon dried oregano
- Salt and freshly ground black pepper, to taste
- Grated Parmesan cheese, for serving
- Fresh basil leaves, torn, for garnish (optional)

Instructions:

1. To make the pici pasta, place the flour on a clean work surface and make a well in the center. Pour the warm water, olive oil, and a pinch of salt into the well. Using a fork or your fingers, gradually incorporate the flour into the liquid until a dough forms.
2. Knead the dough for about 5-7 minutes until it becomes smooth and elastic. If the dough is too dry, add a little more water. If it's too sticky, add a little more flour.
3. Divide the dough into small portions and roll each portion into long ropes, about 1/4 inch thick. Cut the ropes into pieces about 2 inches long. Roll each piece between your palms to create long, thin noodles. Repeat with the remaining dough.

4. Bring a large pot of salted water to a boil. Cook the pici pasta in batches for about 3-4 minutes, or until al dente. Drain the pasta and set aside.
5. While the pasta is cooking, prepare the Tuscan sausage sauce. Heat the olive oil in a large skillet over medium heat. Add the sausage meat and cook, breaking it up with a spoon, until browned and cooked through, about 5-7 minutes.
6. Add the chopped onion to the skillet with the sausage and cook until softened and translucent, about 5 minutes. Add the minced garlic and cook for another 1-2 minutes until fragrant.
7. Pour in the white wine and let it simmer for a couple of minutes to cook off the alcohol.
8. Stir in the crushed tomatoes and dried oregano. Season with salt and freshly ground black pepper to taste. Let the sauce simmer for about 10-15 minutes, stirring occasionally, until it has thickened slightly and the flavors have melded together.
9. Add the cooked pici pasta to the skillet with the Tuscan sausage sauce. Toss everything together until the pasta is well coated in the sauce.
10. Divide the Pici with Tuscan Sausage Sauce among serving plates. Serve hot, garnished with grated Parmesan cheese and torn fresh basil leaves, if desired.
11. Enjoy the hearty and flavorful flavors of this Tuscan-inspired pasta dish!

Feel free to adjust the quantities of the ingredients or customize the recipe to suit your taste preferences. You can also add extra ingredients such as chopped bell peppers or mushrooms for added flavor and texture.

Tortellini alla Panna

Ingredients:

- 350g tortellini pasta (cheese-filled or meat-filled)
- 1 tablespoon olive oil
- 2 cloves garlic, minced
- 1 cup heavy cream
- 1/2 cup grated Parmesan cheese
- Salt and freshly ground black pepper, to taste
- Fresh parsley, chopped, for garnish (optional)

Instructions:

1. Bring a large pot of salted water to a boil. Cook the tortellini pasta according to package instructions until al dente. Drain the pasta and set aside.
2. While the pasta is cooking, heat the olive oil in a large skillet over medium heat. Add the minced garlic and sauté for 1-2 minutes until fragrant.
3. Pour in the heavy cream and bring it to a simmer. Let it simmer gently for about 3-5 minutes, stirring occasionally, until slightly thickened.
4. Stir in the grated Parmesan cheese until melted and smooth. Season the sauce with salt and freshly ground black pepper to taste.
5. Add the cooked tortellini pasta to the skillet with the creamy sauce. Toss everything together until the pasta is well coated in the sauce.
6. Divide the Tortellini alla Panna among serving plates. Garnish with chopped fresh parsley, if desired.
7. Serve hot and enjoy the creamy and indulgent flavors of this classic Italian pasta dish!

Feel free to customize the recipe by adding extra ingredients such as cooked chicken, bacon, or mushrooms for added flavor and texture. You can also adjust the consistency of the sauce by adding more or less cream according to your preference.

Mezze Maniche with Gorgonzola Sauce

Ingredients:

- 350g mezze maniche pasta (or any short pasta shape like penne or rigatoni)
- 200g Gorgonzola cheese, crumbled
- 1 cup heavy cream
- 2 tablespoons unsalted butter
- 2 cloves garlic, minced
- Salt and freshly ground black pepper, to taste
- Fresh parsley, chopped, for garnish (optional)
- Grated Parmesan cheese, for serving (optional)

Instructions:

1. Bring a large pot of salted water to a boil. Cook the mezze maniche pasta according to package instructions until al dente. Drain the pasta and set aside.
2. While the pasta is cooking, prepare the Gorgonzola sauce. In a large skillet, melt the butter over medium heat. Add the minced garlic and sauté for 1-2 minutes until fragrant.
3. Pour in the heavy cream and bring it to a simmer. Let it simmer gently for about 3-5 minutes, stirring occasionally, until slightly thickened.
4. Reduce the heat to low and add the crumbled Gorgonzola cheese to the skillet. Stir until the cheese is melted and the sauce is smooth and creamy. Season with salt and freshly ground black pepper to taste.
5. Add the cooked mezze maniche pasta to the skillet with the Gorgonzola sauce. Toss everything together until the pasta is well coated in the sauce.
6. Divide the Mezze Maniche with Gorgonzola Sauce among serving plates. Garnish with chopped fresh parsley and grated Parmesan cheese, if desired.
7. Serve hot and enjoy the indulgent flavors of this creamy and cheesy pasta dish!

Feel free to customize the recipe by adding extra ingredients such as cooked chicken, crispy bacon, or sautéed mushrooms for added flavor and texture. You can also adjust the intensity of the Gorgonzola flavor by using more or less cheese according to your preference.

Spaghetti alla Nerano

Ingredients:

- 350g spaghetti pasta
- 2 large zucchini, thinly sliced into rounds
- 2 cloves garlic, minced
- 1/2 cup grated Parmesan cheese
- 1/4 cup grated Pecorino Romano cheese
- Fresh basil leaves, torn
- Salt and freshly ground black pepper, to taste
- Extra-virgin olive oil, for frying and drizzling

Instructions:

1. Bring a large pot of salted water to a boil. Cook the spaghetti pasta according to package instructions until al dente. Reserve about 1 cup of pasta water, then drain the pasta and set aside.
2. While the pasta is cooking, heat some olive oil in a large skillet over medium heat. Fry the sliced zucchini rounds in batches until golden brown and crispy on both sides. Remove the fried zucchini from the skillet and drain on paper towels to remove excess oil.
3. In the same skillet, add a little more olive oil if needed, then add the minced garlic. Sauté for 1-2 minutes until fragrant.
4. Return the fried zucchini slices to the skillet with the garlic. Season with salt and freshly ground black pepper to taste. Use a wooden spoon to gently mash the zucchini until it forms a coarse paste.
5. Add the cooked spaghetti pasta to the skillet with the zucchini mixture. Toss everything together, adding some of the reserved pasta water as needed to create a creamy sauce that coats the pasta.
6. Remove the skillet from the heat and add the grated Parmesan cheese and grated Pecorino Romano cheese. Toss again until the cheese is melted and the sauce is well combined.
7. Divide the Spaghetti alla Nerano among serving plates. Garnish with torn fresh basil leaves and an extra drizzle of olive oil, if desired.
8. Serve hot and enjoy the simple yet flavorful taste of this classic Italian pasta dish!

Feel free to adjust the quantities of the ingredients or customize the recipe to suit your taste preferences. You can also add a pinch of red pepper flakes for a hint of heat, or top the dish with additional grated cheese for extra richness.

Farfalle with Smoked Salmon and Cream Sauce

Ingredients:

- 350g farfalle pasta
- 200g smoked salmon, chopped into bite-sized pieces
- 1 cup heavy cream
- 2 tablespoons unsalted butter
- 2 cloves garlic, minced
- 1/4 cup dry white wine (optional)
- Zest of 1 lemon
- Juice of 1/2 lemon
- 2 tablespoons chopped fresh dill
- Salt and freshly ground black pepper, to taste
- Grated Parmesan cheese, for serving (optional)

Instructions:

1. Bring a large pot of salted water to a boil. Cook the farfalle pasta according to package instructions until al dente. Drain the pasta and set aside.
2. In a large skillet, melt the butter over medium heat. Add the minced garlic and sauté for 1-2 minutes until fragrant.
3. If using, pour in the dry white wine and let it simmer for a couple of minutes to cook off the alcohol.
4. Reduce the heat to low and pour in the heavy cream. Stir well to combine.
5. Add the chopped smoked salmon to the skillet and let it simmer gently in the cream sauce for about 2-3 minutes, just until heated through.
6. Stir in the lemon zest, lemon juice, and chopped fresh dill. Season the sauce with salt and freshly ground black pepper to taste.
7. Add the cooked farfalle pasta to the skillet with the smoked salmon cream sauce. Toss everything together until the pasta is well coated in the sauce.
8. Divide the Farfalle with Smoked Salmon and Cream Sauce among serving plates. Garnish with additional chopped fresh dill and grated Parmesan cheese, if desired.
9. Serve hot and enjoy the delicious flavors of this elegant pasta dish!

Feel free to adjust the quantities of the ingredients or customize the recipe to suit your taste preferences. You can also add a splash of chicken broth or seafood broth for extra flavor, or garnish with a sprinkle of red pepper flakes for a hint of heat.

Ravioli di Zucca (Pumpkin Ravioli)

Ingredients:

For the pasta dough:

- 2 cups all-purpose flour
- 3 large eggs
- 1 tablespoon olive oil
- Pinch of salt

For the pumpkin filling:

- 1 cup pumpkin puree (homemade or canned)
- 1/2 cup grated Parmesan cheese
- 1/4 teaspoon ground nutmeg
- Salt and freshly ground black pepper, to taste

For the sauce:

- 4 tablespoons unsalted butter
- 2 cloves garlic, minced
- Fresh sage leaves, chopped
- Salt and freshly ground black pepper, to taste
- Grated Parmesan cheese, for serving

Instructions:

1. To make the pasta dough, mound the flour on a clean work surface and create a well in the center. Crack the eggs into the well and add the olive oil and a pinch of salt. Using a fork, gradually incorporate the flour into the eggs until a dough forms.

2. Knead the dough for about 10 minutes until it becomes smooth and elastic. Wrap the dough in plastic wrap and let it rest at room temperature for at least 30 minutes.
3. While the dough is resting, prepare the pumpkin filling. In a mixing bowl, combine the pumpkin puree, grated Parmesan cheese, ground nutmeg, salt, and pepper. Mix until well combined. Adjust seasoning to taste.
4. Once the dough has rested, divide it into smaller portions. Roll out each portion of dough into a thin sheet using a rolling pin or pasta machine.
5. Place small spoonfuls of the pumpkin filling evenly spaced apart on one sheet of pasta dough. Be careful not to overfill.
6. Brush a little water around each mound of filling, then carefully place another sheet of pasta dough on top. Press down gently around each mound of filling to seal the ravioli.
7. Use a sharp knife or a fluted pastry cutter to cut out the individual ravioli. Make sure to press down firmly around the edges to ensure they are well sealed.
8. Bring a large pot of salted water to a boil. Carefully drop the ravioli into the boiling water and cook for about 2-3 minutes, or until they float to the surface. Remove the cooked ravioli with a slotted spoon and set aside.
9. While the ravioli are cooking, prepare the sauce. In a large skillet, melt the butter over medium heat. Add the minced garlic and chopped sage leaves. Cook for 1-2 minutes until fragrant.
10. Add the cooked ravioli to the skillet with the butter sauce. Gently toss everything together until the ravioli are evenly coated in the sauce. Season with salt and freshly ground black pepper to taste.
11. Divide the Ravioli di Zucca among serving plates. Serve hot, garnished with grated Parmesan cheese.
12. Enjoy the delicious flavors of homemade Pumpkin Ravioli!

Feel free to adjust the recipe by adding a touch of cream to the sauce for extra richness, or by incorporating other seasonings such as cinnamon or cloves to the pumpkin filling for added warmth.

Fettuccine with Shrimp Scampi

Ingredients:

- 350g fettuccine pasta
- 400g large shrimp, peeled and deveined
- 4 tablespoons unsalted butter
- 4 tablespoons olive oil
- 4 cloves garlic, minced
- 1/4 teaspoon red pepper flakes (adjust to taste)
- Zest of 1 lemon
- Juice of 1 lemon
- 1/4 cup dry white wine (optional)
- Salt and freshly ground black pepper, to taste
- Chopped fresh parsley, for garnish
- Grated Parmesan cheese, for serving (optional)

Instructions:

1. Bring a large pot of salted water to a boil. Cook the fettuccine pasta according to package instructions until al dente. Drain the pasta and set aside.
2. While the pasta is cooking, heat 2 tablespoons of butter and 2 tablespoons of olive oil in a large skillet over medium heat. Add the minced garlic and red pepper flakes. Sauté for about 1-2 minutes until fragrant.
3. Add the shrimp to the skillet in a single layer. Cook for 2-3 minutes on each side until pink and opaque. Remove the cooked shrimp from the skillet and set aside.
4. In the same skillet, add the remaining 2 tablespoons of butter and 2 tablespoons of olive oil. If using, pour in the dry white wine and let it simmer for a couple of minutes to cook off the alcohol.
5. Add the cooked fettuccine pasta to the skillet with the garlic and butter sauce. Toss to coat the pasta evenly.
6. Return the cooked shrimp to the skillet. Add the lemon zest and lemon juice. Toss everything together until well combined.
7. Season the Fettuccine with Shrimp Scampi with salt and freshly ground black pepper to taste.
8. Garnish the dish with chopped fresh parsley and grated Parmesan cheese, if desired.

9. Serve hot and enjoy the delightful flavors of this classic pasta dish!

Feel free to customize the recipe by adding additional ingredients such as cherry tomatoes or spinach for extra flavor and nutrition. You can also adjust the amount of garlic and red pepper flakes according to your taste preferences.

Penne alla Vodka

Ingredients:

- 350g penne pasta
- 2 tablespoons olive oil
- 2 cloves garlic, minced
- 1/4 teaspoon red pepper flakes (optional, adjust to taste)
- 1/2 cup vodka
- 1 can (400g) crushed tomatoes
- 1/2 cup heavy cream
- Salt and freshly ground black pepper, to taste
- Fresh basil leaves, chopped, for garnish (optional)
- Grated Parmesan cheese, for serving (optional)

Instructions:

1. Bring a large pot of salted water to a boil. Cook the penne pasta according to package instructions until al dente. Drain the pasta and set aside.
2. While the pasta is cooking, heat the olive oil in a large skillet over medium heat. Add the minced garlic and red pepper flakes, if using. Sauté for 1-2 minutes until fragrant.
3. Pour in the vodka and let it simmer for a couple of minutes to cook off the alcohol.
4. Stir in the crushed tomatoes and bring the sauce to a simmer. Let it cook for about 10-15 minutes, stirring occasionally, until slightly thickened.
5. Reduce the heat to low and stir in the heavy cream. Let the sauce simmer for another 5-7 minutes, stirring occasionally, until it thickens slightly.
6. Season the Penne alla Vodka sauce with salt and freshly ground black pepper to taste.
7. Add the cooked penne pasta to the skillet with the vodka sauce. Toss everything together until the pasta is well coated in the sauce.
8. Divide the Penne alla Vodka among serving plates. Garnish with chopped fresh basil leaves and grated Parmesan cheese, if desired.
9. Serve hot and enjoy the creamy and flavorful Penne alla Vodka!

Feel free to adjust the recipe by adding cooked pancetta or crispy bacon for extra flavor, or by incorporating a splash of chicken broth for additional depth. You can also garnish the dish with additional red pepper flakes for a spicy kick, or with chopped parsley for a fresh touch.

Linguine with Lobster Sauce

Ingredients:

- 350g linguine pasta
- 2 lobster tails, shells removed and meat chopped into bite-sized pieces
- 4 tablespoons unsalted butter
- 4 tablespoons olive oil
- 4 cloves garlic, minced
- 1/2 cup dry white wine
- 1 cup seafood or lobster stock (or chicken broth)
- 1 cup heavy cream
- 2 tablespoons tomato paste
- Salt and freshly ground black pepper, to taste
- Chopped fresh parsley, for garnish
- Grated Parmesan cheese, for serving (optional)

Instructions:

1. Bring a large pot of salted water to a boil. Cook the linguine pasta according to package instructions until al dente. Drain the pasta and set aside.
2. While the pasta is cooking, heat 2 tablespoons of butter and 2 tablespoons of olive oil in a large skillet over medium heat. Add the minced garlic and sauté for 1-2 minutes until fragrant.
3. Add the chopped lobster meat to the skillet and cook for 2-3 minutes until it starts to turn opaque.
4. Pour in the dry white wine and let it simmer for a couple of minutes to cook off the alcohol.
5. Add the seafood or lobster stock (or chicken broth) to the skillet. Bring the mixture to a simmer and let it cook for about 5-7 minutes to reduce slightly.
6. Stir in the heavy cream and tomato paste. Let the sauce simmer for another 5-7 minutes until it thickens slightly.
7. Season the Linguine with Lobster Sauce with salt and freshly ground black pepper to taste.
8. Add the cooked linguine pasta to the skillet with the lobster sauce. Toss everything together until the pasta is well coated in the sauce.

9. Divide the Linguine with Lobster Sauce among serving plates. Garnish with chopped fresh parsley and grated Parmesan cheese, if desired.
10. Serve hot and enjoy the luxurious and indulgent flavors of this elegant pasta dish!

Feel free to customize the recipe by adding additional seafood such as shrimp or scallops for extra variety and flavor. You can also add a pinch of red pepper flakes for a hint of heat, or garnish with lemon zest for a fresh touch.

Lasagna Verde

Ingredients:

For the Spinach Pasta Sheets:

- 300g fresh spinach leaves, washed and stems removed
- 3 large eggs
- 400g all-purpose flour
- Pinch of salt

For the Béchamel Sauce:

- 4 tablespoons unsalted butter
- 1/4 cup all-purpose flour
- 4 cups whole milk
- Salt, to taste
- Freshly grated nutmeg, to taste

For the Tomato Meat Sauce:

- 500g ground beef or pork
- 1 onion, finely chopped
- 2 cloves garlic, minced
- 1 can (400g) crushed tomatoes
- 2 tablespoons tomato paste
- 1 teaspoon dried oregano
- Salt and freshly ground black pepper, to taste

Additional Layers:

- 1 cup grated Parmesan cheese
- 2 cups shredded mozzarella cheese

Instructions:

1. To make the Spinach Pasta Sheets:
     - Blanch the spinach leaves in boiling water for about 1 minute, then transfer them to a bowl of ice water to cool. Drain well and squeeze out any excess water.
     - In a blender or food processor, puree the blanched spinach leaves with the eggs until smooth.
     - On a clean work surface, mound the flour and make a well in the center. Pour the spinach mixture into the well.
     - Using a fork or your fingers, gradually incorporate the flour into the spinach mixture until a dough forms.
     - Knead the dough for about 5-7 minutes until smooth and elastic. Wrap in plastic wrap and let it rest for 30 minutes.
     - Roll out the dough into thin sheets using a pasta machine or rolling pin. Cut the sheets into rectangles to fit your baking dish.
2. To make the Béchamel Sauce:
     - In a saucepan, melt the butter over medium heat. Add the flour and cook, stirring constantly, for 1-2 minutes to make a roux.
     - Gradually whisk in the milk until smooth. Cook the sauce, stirring constantly, until thickened.
     - Season with salt and nutmeg to taste. Remove from heat and set aside.
3. To make the Tomato Meat Sauce:
     - In a large skillet, cook the ground meat over medium heat until browned. Add the chopped onion and minced garlic, and cook until softened.
     - Stir in the crushed tomatoes, tomato paste, dried oregano, salt, and pepper. Let the sauce simmer for about 15-20 minutes until thickened.
4. Preheat your oven to 375°F (190°C). Grease a baking dish with butter or cooking spray.
5. To assemble the Lasagna Verde:
     - Spread a thin layer of the tomato meat sauce on the bottom of the prepared baking dish.
     - Place a layer of spinach pasta sheets on top of the sauce.
     - Spread a layer of béchamel sauce over the pasta sheets, followed by a layer of tomato meat sauce. Sprinkle with grated Parmesan and mozzarella cheese.
     - Repeat the layers until all ingredients are used, ending with a layer of tomato meat sauce and cheese on top.

6. Cover the baking dish with aluminum foil and bake in the preheated oven for 25-30 minutes.
7. Remove the foil and bake for an additional 10-15 minutes until the cheese is golden and bubbly.
8. Let the Lasagna Verde rest for a few minutes before slicing and serving.
9. Enjoy the delicious layers of spinach pasta, creamy béchamel sauce, and savory tomato meat sauce in this classic Italian dish!

Feel free to adjust the recipe by adding other ingredients such as ricotta cheese or mushrooms to the layers for extra flavor and texture. You can also make the spinach pasta and sauces ahead of time to streamline the assembly process.

Tagliatelle with Truffle Cream Sauce

Ingredients:

- 350g tagliatelle pasta
- 2 tablespoons unsalted butter
- 2 tablespoons olive oil
- 2 cloves garlic, minced
- 1/4 cup dry white wine
- 1 cup heavy cream
- 2-3 tablespoons truffle paste or truffle oil (adjust to taste)
- Salt and freshly ground black pepper, to taste
- Grated Parmesan cheese, for serving
- Fresh parsley, chopped, for garnish (optional)

Instructions:

1. Bring a large pot of salted water to a boil. Cook the tagliatelle pasta according to package instructions until al dente. Drain the pasta and set aside.
2. While the pasta is cooking, heat the butter and olive oil in a large skillet over medium heat. Add the minced garlic and sauté for 1-2 minutes until fragrant.
3. Pour in the dry white wine and let it simmer for a couple of minutes to cook off the alcohol.
4. Reduce the heat to low and pour in the heavy cream. Stir well to combine.
5. Add the truffle paste or truffle oil to the skillet, stirring until well incorporated into the cream sauce. Adjust the amount according to your taste preference.
6. Let the sauce simmer gently for about 5-7 minutes until it thickens slightly. Season with salt and freshly ground black pepper to taste.
7. Add the cooked tagliatelle pasta to the skillet with the truffle cream sauce. Toss everything together until the pasta is well coated in the sauce.
8. Divide the Tagliatelle with Truffle Cream Sauce among serving plates. Sprinkle with grated Parmesan cheese and chopped fresh parsley, if desired.
9. Serve hot and enjoy the luxurious and indulgent flavors of this elegant pasta dish!

Feel free to garnish the dish with additional truffle shavings for extra presentation and flavor. You can also add cooked mushrooms or crispy pancetta for additional texture and depth of flavor.

Gnocchi alla Romana

Ingredients:

For the Gnocchi:

- 1 liter whole milk
- 250g semolina flour
- 100g grated Parmesan cheese
- 100g unsalted butter
- Salt, to taste
- Pinch of nutmeg (optional)

For the Baking Dish:

- Butter, for greasing
- Additional grated Parmesan cheese, for sprinkling

Instructions:

1. In a large saucepan, bring the milk to a simmer over medium heat. Season with salt and a pinch of nutmeg, if using.
2. Gradually whisk in the semolina flour, stirring constantly to prevent lumps from forming.
3. Continue to cook the mixture, stirring constantly, until it thickens and pulls away from the sides of the pan, about 5-7 minutes.
4. Remove the pan from the heat and stir in the grated Parmesan cheese and butter until melted and well combined.
5. Transfer the mixture to a greased baking dish, spreading it out evenly to form a smooth layer. Smooth the surface with a spatula or the back of a spoon.
6. Allow the mixture to cool slightly, then cover and refrigerate until firm, about 1-2 hours or overnight.
7. Once the mixture has set, preheat your oven to 200°C (400°F).

8. Using a round cookie cutter or a glass, cut out individual circles of the semolina mixture and arrange them in a single layer in a greased baking dish, slightly overlapping each other.
9. Sprinkle the top with additional grated Parmesan cheese.
10. Bake in the preheated oven for 20-25 minutes, or until the gnocchi are golden and crispy on top.
11. Serve the Gnocchi alla Romana hot, straight from the oven.
12. Enjoy the creamy, cheesy goodness of this classic Italian dish!

Feel free to customize the dish by adding herbs such as chopped fresh parsley or thyme to the semolina mixture before baking. You can also serve it with a tomato sauce or a drizzle of melted butter for extra flavor.

Farfalle with Asparagus and Prosciutto

Ingredients:

- 350g farfalle pasta
- 200g asparagus, trimmed and cut into bite-sized pieces
- 100g prosciutto, thinly sliced and chopped
- 2 tablespoons unsalted butter
- 2 cloves garlic, minced
- 1 cup heavy cream
- 1/2 cup grated Parmesan cheese
- Salt and freshly ground black pepper, to taste
- Fresh parsley, chopped, for garnish (optional)

Instructions:

1. Bring a large pot of salted water to a boil. Cook the farfalle pasta according to package instructions until al dente. During the last 2 minutes of cooking, add the asparagus to the boiling water. Drain the pasta and asparagus and set aside.
2. While the pasta is cooking, heat the butter in a large skillet over medium heat. Add the minced garlic and cook for 1-2 minutes until fragrant.
3. Add the chopped prosciutto to the skillet and cook for 2-3 minutes until it starts to crisp up slightly.
4. Pour in the heavy cream and bring it to a simmer. Let it simmer gently for about 3-5 minutes, stirring occasionally, until slightly thickened.
5. Stir in the grated Parmesan cheese until melted and smooth. Season the sauce with salt and freshly ground black pepper to taste.
6. Add the cooked farfalle pasta and asparagus to the skillet with the cream sauce. Toss everything together until the pasta and asparagus are well coated in the sauce.
7. Divide the Farfalle with Asparagus and Prosciutto among serving plates. Garnish with chopped fresh parsley, if desired.
8. Serve hot and enjoy the delicious combination of flavors in this pasta dish!

Feel free to customize the recipe by adding other ingredients such as cherry tomatoes or mushrooms for extra flavor and texture. You can also adjust the consistency of the sauce by adding more or less heavy cream according to your preference.

Cannelloni al Forno

Ingredients:

For the Cannelloni:

- 250g cannelloni tubes (dried or fresh)
- 500g ricotta cheese
- 200g spinach, cooked and chopped (or use frozen spinach, thawed and drained)
- 100g grated Parmesan cheese
- 1 egg
- Salt and freshly ground black pepper, to taste
- Pinch of nutmeg (optional)

For the Tomato Sauce:

- 2 tablespoons olive oil
- 1 onion, finely chopped
- 2 cloves garlic, minced
- 1 can (400g) crushed tomatoes
- 2 tablespoons tomato paste
- 1 teaspoon dried oregano
- Salt and freshly ground black pepper, to taste

For the Béchamel Sauce:

- 4 tablespoons unsalted butter
- 1/4 cup all-purpose flour
- 4 cups whole milk
- Salt, to taste
- Freshly grated nutmeg, to taste

Instructions:

1. Preheat your oven to 180°C (350°F). Grease a baking dish with butter or cooking spray.
2. To make the Cannelloni filling:
    - In a large mixing bowl, combine the ricotta cheese, chopped spinach, grated Parmesan cheese, egg, salt, pepper, and nutmeg (if using). Mix until well combined.
3. To make the Tomato Sauce:
    - In a saucepan, heat the olive oil over medium heat. Add the chopped onion and garlic, and cook until softened.
    - Stir in the crushed tomatoes, tomato paste, dried oregano, salt, and pepper. Simmer the sauce for about 10-15 minutes until thickened slightly.
4. To make the Béchamel Sauce:
    - In a separate saucepan, melt the butter over medium heat. Add the flour and cook, stirring constantly, for 1-2 minutes to make a roux.
    - Gradually whisk in the milk until smooth. Cook the sauce, stirring constantly, until thickened.
    - Season with salt and freshly grated nutmeg to taste.
5. To assemble the Cannelloni:
    - Spoon a thin layer of tomato sauce onto the bottom of the prepared baking dish.
    - Fill each cannelloni tube with the ricotta and spinach mixture using a piping bag or a spoon, and arrange them in a single layer in the baking dish.
    - Pour the remaining tomato sauce over the top of the cannelloni tubes, spreading it out evenly.
    - Pour the béchamel sauce over the top of the tomato sauce, spreading it out evenly.
6. Cover the baking dish with aluminum foil and bake in the preheated oven for 30 minutes.
7. Remove the foil and bake for an additional 10-15 minutes, or until the top is golden and bubbly.
8. Let the Cannelloni al Forno rest for a few minutes before serving.
9. Enjoy the delicious flavors of this classic Italian baked pasta dish!

Feel free to garnish the Cannelloni al Forno with additional grated Parmesan cheese and chopped fresh parsley before serving, if desired.

Orecchiette with Broccoli and Anchovies

Ingredients:

- 350g orecchiette pasta
- 1 head broccoli, cut into small florets
- 4 tablespoons extra virgin olive oil
- 4 cloves garlic, minced
- 4-6 anchovy fillets, chopped
- 1/4 teaspoon red pepper flakes (optional)
- Salt, to taste
- Freshly ground black pepper, to taste
- Grated Parmesan cheese, for serving (optional)

Instructions:

1. Bring a large pot of salted water to a boil. Cook the orecchiette pasta according to package instructions until al dente. During the last 2 minutes of cooking, add the broccoli florets to the boiling water. Drain the pasta and broccoli and set aside.
2. While the pasta is cooking, heat the olive oil in a large skillet over medium heat. Add the minced garlic and cook for 1-2 minutes until fragrant.
3. Add the chopped anchovy fillets to the skillet and cook, stirring, until they dissolve into the oil, about 2-3 minutes.
4. If using, add the red pepper flakes to the skillet and cook for an additional 1 minute.
5. Add the cooked orecchiette pasta and broccoli to the skillet with the anchovy mixture. Toss everything together until well combined.
6. Season the Orecchiette with Broccoli and Anchovies with salt and freshly ground black pepper to taste.
7. Divide the pasta among serving plates. Serve hot, sprinkled with grated Parmesan cheese, if desired.
8. Enjoy the flavorful combination of tender pasta, crisp broccoli, and savory anchovies!

Feel free to adjust the recipe by adding sliced black olives or toasted pine nuts for extra flavor and texture. You can also drizzle with a squeeze of lemon juice before serving for a fresh touch.

Spaghetti alla Siciliana

Ingredients:

- 350g spaghetti
- 4 tablespoons extra virgin olive oil
- 2 cloves garlic, thinly sliced
- 1 small red onion, finely chopped
- 1 can (400g) crushed tomatoes
- 1/4 cup pitted black olives, sliced
- 2 tablespoons capers, rinsed and drained
- 1 tablespoon dried oregano
- 1/2 teaspoon red pepper flakes (optional)
- Salt, to taste
- Freshly ground black pepper, to taste
- Fresh basil leaves, torn, for garnish
- Grated Pecorino Romano cheese, for serving (optional)

Instructions:

1. Cook the spaghetti in a large pot of salted boiling water until al dente, according to package instructions. Drain the pasta, reserving a small amount of pasta water, and set aside.
2. In a large skillet, heat the olive oil over medium heat. Add the sliced garlic and cook until golden and fragrant, about 1-2 minutes.
3. Add the chopped red onion to the skillet and cook until softened, about 3-4 minutes.
4. Stir in the crushed tomatoes, black olives, capers, dried oregano, and red pepper flakes (if using). Season with salt and black pepper to taste. Allow the sauce to simmer for about 10 minutes, stirring occasionally, until it thickens slightly.
5. Add the cooked spaghetti to the skillet with the sauce. Toss everything together until the pasta is evenly coated in the sauce. If the sauce is too thick, add a splash of reserved pasta water to loosen it up.
6. Divide the Spaghetti alla Siciliana among serving plates. Garnish with torn fresh basil leaves and grated Pecorino Romano cheese, if desired.
7. Serve hot and enjoy the delicious flavors of Sicily!

Feel free to customize the recipe by adding other ingredients such as anchovies, pine nuts, or raisins for extra flavor and texture. You can also use fresh cherry tomatoes instead of crushed tomatoes for a lighter sauce.

Rigatoni con Pesto Trapanese

Ingredients:

For the Pesto Trapanese:

- 200g cherry tomatoes, halved
- 50g almonds, toasted
- 2 cloves garlic, minced
- 1 cup fresh basil leaves
- 4 tablespoons extra virgin olive oil
- Salt, to taste
- Freshly ground black pepper, to taste
- Grated Parmesan cheese, for serving (optional)

For the Rigatoni:

- 350g rigatoni pasta
- Salt, for cooking pasta

Instructions:

1. Bring a large pot of salted water to a boil. Cook the rigatoni pasta according to package instructions until al dente. Reserve 1/2 cup of pasta cooking water, then drain the pasta and set aside.
2. While the pasta is cooking, prepare the Pesto Trapanese. In a food processor or blender, combine the cherry tomatoes, toasted almonds, minced garlic, and fresh basil leaves. Pulse until coarsely chopped.
3. With the food processor running, gradually drizzle in the olive oil until the mixture forms a smooth sauce. Season with salt and black pepper to taste.
4. In a large skillet, heat the Pesto Trapanese sauce over medium heat until warmed through.
5. Add the cooked rigatoni pasta to the skillet with the Pesto Trapanese sauce. Toss everything together until the pasta is evenly coated with the sauce. If the sauce is too thick, add a splash of reserved pasta cooking water to loosen it up.

6. Divide the Rigatoni con Pesto Trapanese among serving plates. Serve hot, sprinkled with grated Parmesan cheese if desired.
7. Enjoy the delicious flavors of Sicily in this simple and satisfying pasta dish!

Feel free to adjust the recipe by adding additional ingredients such as sun-dried tomatoes or red pepper flakes for extra flavor. You can also garnish the dish with additional toasted almonds or fresh basil leaves for a decorative touch.

Pappardelle with Rabbit Ragu

Ingredients:

For the Rabbit Ragu:

- 1 rabbit, cut into pieces (about 2-3 pounds)
- 2 tablespoons olive oil
- 1 onion, finely chopped
- 2 carrots, finely chopped
- 2 celery stalks, finely chopped
- 4 cloves garlic, minced
- 1 can (400g) crushed tomatoes
- 1/2 cup dry white wine
- 1 cup chicken or vegetable broth
- 2 bay leaves
- 1 teaspoon dried thyme
- Salt and pepper to taste
- Fresh parsley for garnish (optional)

For the Pappardelle:

- 400g pappardelle pasta
- Salt for boiling water

Instructions:

1. Heat the olive oil in a large Dutch oven or heavy-bottomed pot over medium-high heat. Add the rabbit pieces and brown them on all sides, about 5 minutes per side. Remove the rabbit from the pot and set aside.
2. In the same pot, add the chopped onion, carrots, and celery. Cook, stirring occasionally, until the vegetables are softened, about 5-7 minutes.
3. Add the minced garlic to the pot and cook for another minute until fragrant.

4. Return the browned rabbit pieces to the pot. Pour in the crushed tomatoes, white wine, chicken or vegetable broth, bay leaves, and dried thyme. Season with salt and pepper to taste.
5. Bring the mixture to a simmer, then reduce the heat to low. Cover the pot and let the rabbit ragu simmer gently for 2-3 hours, stirring occasionally, until the meat is tender and falls off the bone.
6. While the ragu is simmering, cook the pappardelle pasta according to the package instructions in a large pot of salted boiling water until al dente. Drain the cooked pasta and set aside.
7. Once the rabbit is tender, remove the pieces from the pot and shred the meat using two forks, discarding any bones and cartilage.
8. Return the shredded rabbit meat to the pot and stir it into the sauce. Simmer for another 10-15 minutes to allow the flavors to meld together.
9. Taste the ragu and adjust the seasoning with salt and pepper if needed.
10. Serve the Pappardelle with Rabbit Ragu hot, spooning the ragu over the cooked pappardelle pasta.
11. Garnish with fresh parsley if desired.
12. Enjoy your hearty and flavorful Pappardelle with Rabbit Ragu, a comforting and satisfying Italian-inspired dish!

Conchiglie alla Fiorentina

Ingredients:

- 400g conchiglie pasta
- 200g fresh spinach leaves, washed and chopped
- 2 tablespoons olive oil
- 2 cloves garlic, minced
- 1 onion, finely chopped
- 200ml heavy cream
- 1 cup grated Parmesan cheese
- Salt and pepper to taste
- Pinch of nutmeg (optional)
- Fresh parsley for garnish (optional)

Instructions:

1. Cook the conchiglie pasta according to the package instructions in a large pot of salted boiling water until al dente. Drain the cooked pasta and set aside.
2. In a large skillet or frying pan, heat the olive oil over medium heat. Add the minced garlic and chopped onion, and sauté until softened and fragrant, about 3-4 minutes.
3. Add the chopped spinach leaves to the skillet and cook until wilted, about 2-3 minutes.
4. Pour in the heavy cream and stir to combine. Let the mixture simmer gently for 2-3 minutes.
5. Stir in the grated Parmesan cheese until melted and smooth. Season the sauce with salt, pepper, and a pinch of nutmeg, if using. Taste and adjust the seasoning as needed.
6. Add the cooked conchiglie pasta to the skillet with the spinach and cream sauce. Toss well to coat the pasta evenly with the sauce.
7. Cook for another minute or two until the pasta is heated through and well coated with the sauce.
8. Remove the skillet from heat and transfer the Conchiglie alla Fiorentina to serving plates.
9. Garnish with fresh parsley, if desired, and serve hot.

10. Enjoy your creamy and flavorful Conchiglie alla Fiorentina, a delicious and comforting Italian pasta dish!

Paccheri with Eggplant and Ricotta Salata

Ingredients:

- 400g paccheri pasta
- 1 large eggplant, diced
- 3 tablespoons olive oil
- 2 cloves garlic, minced
- 1 onion, finely chopped
- 1 can (400g) diced tomatoes
- 1/2 teaspoon dried oregano
- 1/2 teaspoon dried basil
- Salt and pepper to taste
- 150g ricotta salata cheese, grated or crumbled
- Fresh basil leaves for garnish (optional)

Instructions:

1. Cook the paccheri pasta according to the package instructions in a large pot of salted boiling water until al dente. Drain the cooked pasta and set aside.
2. While the pasta is cooking, heat 2 tablespoons of olive oil in a large skillet or frying pan over medium heat. Add the diced eggplant and cook until golden brown and tender, about 8-10 minutes. Remove the cooked eggplant from the skillet and set aside.
3. In the same skillet, heat the remaining 1 tablespoon of olive oil over medium heat. Add the minced garlic and chopped onion, and sauté until softened and fragrant, about 3-4 minutes.
4. Stir in the diced tomatoes, dried oregano, and dried basil. Season with salt and pepper to taste. Let the sauce simmer for 5-7 minutes, allowing the flavors to meld together.
5. Return the cooked eggplant to the skillet and stir to combine with the tomato sauce. Cook for another 2-3 minutes to heat through.
6. Add the cooked paccheri pasta to the skillet with the eggplant and tomato sauce. Toss well to coat the pasta evenly with the sauce.
7. Remove the skillet from heat and transfer the Paccheri with Eggplant and Ricotta Salata to serving plates.

8. Sprinkle the grated or crumbled ricotta salata cheese over the top of each serving.
9. Garnish with fresh basil leaves, if desired, and serve hot.
10. Enjoy your delicious and flavorful Paccheri with Eggplant and Ricotta Salata, a delightful Italian pasta dish that's sure to impress!

Cacio e Pepe with Lemon Zest

Ingredients:

- 400g spaghetti or tonnarelli pasta
- 1 cup freshly grated Pecorino Romano cheese
- 2 teaspoons freshly ground black pepper
- Zest of 1 lemon
- 2 tablespoons unsalted butter
- Salt to taste
- Extra virgin olive oil (optional)

Instructions:

1. Cook the pasta in a large pot of salted boiling water until al dente, according to the package instructions. Reserve about 1 cup of pasta cooking water before draining the pasta.
2. While the pasta is cooking, prepare the sauce. In a large skillet or frying pan, melt the butter over medium heat.
3. Add the freshly ground black pepper to the melted butter and toast it for about 1-2 minutes, stirring constantly, until fragrant.
4. Once the pepper is toasted, add about 1/2 cup of the reserved pasta cooking water to the skillet and bring it to a simmer.
5. Add the cooked pasta to the skillet with the pepper and pasta cooking water. Toss the pasta in the skillet, coating it with the pepper-infused water and butter.
6. Gradually add the freshly grated Pecorino Romano cheese to the pasta, tossing continuously, until the cheese melts and forms a creamy sauce. If the sauce seems too thick, add more pasta cooking water as needed to loosen it up.
7. Once the cheese has melted and the sauce is creamy, remove the skillet from heat.
8. Stir in the lemon zest, ensuring it is evenly distributed throughout the pasta.
9. Taste the Cacio e Pepe and adjust the seasoning with salt if needed. Be mindful of the saltiness of the Pecorino Romano cheese.
10. If desired, drizzle a little extra virgin olive oil over the pasta just before serving.
11. Serve the Cacio e Pepe with Lemon Zest hot, garnished with additional black pepper and grated Pecorino Romano cheese if desired.

12. Enjoy your delicious and aromatic Cacio e Pepe with a refreshing hint of lemon zest!

Bucatini with Tuna and Capers

Ingredients:

- 400g bucatini pasta
- 2 tablespoons olive oil
- 2 cloves garlic, minced
- 1 small onion, finely chopped
- 1 can (170g) tuna in olive oil, drained
- 2 tablespoons capers, rinsed and drained
- 1/2 cup cherry tomatoes, halved
- Zest and juice of 1 lemon
- Salt and pepper to taste
- Fresh parsley for garnish (optional)
- Grated Parmesan cheese for serving (optional)

Instructions:

1. Cook the bucatini pasta in a large pot of salted boiling water until al dente, according to the package instructions. Reserve about 1 cup of pasta cooking water before draining the pasta.
2. While the pasta is cooking, heat the olive oil in a large skillet or frying pan over medium heat. Add the minced garlic and chopped onion, and sauté until softened and fragrant, about 3-4 minutes.
3. Add the drained tuna to the skillet, breaking it up into smaller pieces with a spoon. Cook for 2-3 minutes, stirring occasionally.
4. Stir in the capers and cherry tomatoes, and cook for another 2-3 minutes, until the tomatoes begin to soften.
5. Add the cooked bucatini pasta to the skillet with the tuna mixture. Toss well to combine, adding a splash of pasta cooking water if needed to loosen the sauce.
6. Stir in the lemon zest and juice, and season the pasta with salt and pepper to taste. Toss until everything is evenly distributed.
7. Remove the skillet from heat and transfer the Bucatini with Tuna and Capers to serving plates.
8. Garnish with chopped fresh parsley and grated Parmesan cheese, if desired.
9. Serve hot and enjoy your delicious and flavorful Bucatini with Tuna and Capers!

Feel free to adjust the quantities of ingredients to suit your taste preferences, and add a drizzle of extra virgin olive oil before serving for an extra touch of richness.

Strozzapreti with Cherry Tomatoes and Burrata

Ingredients:

- 400g strozzapreti pasta
- 2 tablespoons olive oil
- 2 cloves garlic, minced
- 1 pint (about 300g) cherry tomatoes, halved
- Salt and pepper to taste
- 1 ball of burrata cheese
- Fresh basil leaves for garnish
- Grated Parmesan cheese for serving (optional)

Instructions:

1. Cook the strozzapreti pasta in a large pot of salted boiling water until al dente, according to the package instructions. Reserve about 1 cup of pasta cooking water before draining the pasta.
2. While the pasta is cooking, heat the olive oil in a large skillet or frying pan over medium heat. Add the minced garlic and sauté until fragrant, about 1 minute.
3. Add the cherry tomatoes to the skillet and cook, stirring occasionally, until they start to soften and release their juices, about 5-7 minutes.
4. Season the cherry tomatoes with salt and pepper to taste.
5. Once the cherry tomatoes are cooked, add the cooked strozzapreti pasta to the skillet. Toss the pasta with the cherry tomatoes, coating it evenly with the tomato sauce.
6. If the sauce seems too dry, add a splash of pasta cooking water to loosen it up.
7. Tear the burrata cheese into small pieces and scatter them over the pasta.
8. Garnish the Strozzapreti with Cherry Tomatoes and Burrata with fresh basil leaves.
9. Serve hot, allowing the creamy burrata cheese to melt into the pasta.
10. Optionally, offer grated Parmesan cheese on the side for those who want to add an extra cheesy kick.
11. Enjoy your delicious and creamy Strozzapreti with Cherry Tomatoes and Burrata!

Cavatelli with Rapini and Garlic

Ingredients:

- 400g cavatelli pasta
- 1 bunch rapini (broccoli rabe), washed and trimmed
- 4 cloves garlic, thinly sliced
- 1/4 cup extra virgin olive oil
- Salt to taste
- Red pepper flakes (optional)
- Grated Pecorino Romano cheese for serving (optional)

Instructions:

1. Bring a large pot of salted water to a boil. Add the cavatelli pasta and cook according to the package instructions until al dente. Reserve about 1 cup of pasta cooking water before draining the pasta.
2. While the pasta is cooking, blanch the rapini in a separate pot of boiling salted water for about 2-3 minutes, or until tender. Drain the rapini and set aside.
3. In a large skillet or frying pan, heat the olive oil over medium heat. Add the sliced garlic and red pepper flakes (if using), and sauté until the garlic is golden brown and fragrant, about 1-2 minutes. Be careful not to let the garlic burn.
4. Add the blanched rapini to the skillet with the garlic and olive oil. Cook, stirring occasionally, for another 2-3 minutes, allowing the flavors to meld together.
5. Season the rapini with salt to taste.
6. Add the cooked cavatelli pasta to the skillet with the rapini and garlic. Toss well to combine, adding a splash of pasta cooking water if needed to loosen the sauce.
7. Cook for another minute or two, ensuring the pasta is well coated with the garlic-infused olive oil.
8. Remove the skillet from heat and transfer the Cavatelli with Rapini and Garlic to serving plates.
9. Serve hot, optionally topped with grated Pecorino Romano cheese for an extra burst of flavor.
10. Enjoy your delicious Cavatelli with Rapini and Garlic, a simple yet satisfying Italian dish that celebrates the beauty of fresh ingredients!

Manicotti with Ricotta and Spinach

Ingredients:

For the Manicotti:

- 12 manicotti pasta shells
- 2 cups ricotta cheese
- 1 cup shredded mozzarella cheese
- 1/2 cup grated Parmesan cheese
- 1 cup chopped spinach, cooked and squeezed dry
- 2 cloves garlic, minced
- 1 egg
- 1/4 teaspoon dried oregano
- Salt and pepper to taste

For the Sauce:

- 2 cups marinara sauce
- 1/2 cup shredded mozzarella cheese (for topping)
- Fresh basil leaves for garnish (optional)

Instructions:

1. Preheat your oven to 350°F (175°C). Lightly grease a 9x13-inch baking dish with cooking spray or olive oil.
2. Cook the manicotti pasta shells according to the package instructions until al dente. Drain the cooked pasta and set aside to cool.
3. In a large mixing bowl, combine the ricotta cheese, shredded mozzarella cheese, grated Parmesan cheese, chopped spinach, minced garlic, egg, dried oregano, salt, and pepper. Mix until well combined.
4. Using a spoon or piping bag, carefully fill each cooked manicotti shell with the ricotta-spinach mixture. Arrange the filled manicotti shells in the prepared baking dish.

5. Pour the marinara sauce evenly over the stuffed manicotti shells, covering them completely.
6. Cover the baking dish with aluminum foil and bake in the preheated oven for 25-30 minutes, or until the sauce is bubbly and the manicotti shells are heated through.
7. Remove the foil from the baking dish and sprinkle the remaining shredded mozzarella cheese over the top of the manicotti.
8. Return the baking dish to the oven and bake, uncovered, for an additional 10-15 minutes, or until the cheese is melted and golden brown.
9. Once done, remove the manicotti from the oven and let it cool for a few minutes before serving.
10. Garnish with fresh basil leaves, if desired, and serve hot.
11. Enjoy your delicious Manicotti with Ricotta and Spinach, a comforting and satisfying Italian-inspired dish!

Fusilli with Pistachio Pesto

Ingredients:

For the Pistachio Pesto:

- 1 cup shelled pistachios, lightly toasted
- 2 cups fresh basil leaves
- 2 cloves garlic
- 1/2 cup grated Parmesan cheese
- 1/2 cup extra virgin olive oil
- Salt and pepper to taste

For the Pasta:

- 400g fusilli pasta
- Salt for boiling water
- Grated Parmesan cheese for serving (optional)
- Additional toasted pistachios for garnish (optional)

Instructions:

1. Cook the fusilli pasta in a large pot of salted boiling water according to the package instructions until al dente. Reserve about 1 cup of pasta cooking water before draining the pasta.
2. While the pasta is cooking, prepare the pistachio pesto. In a food processor, combine the toasted pistachios, fresh basil leaves, garlic cloves, and grated Parmesan cheese. Pulse until the ingredients are finely chopped.
3. With the food processor running, gradually drizzle in the extra virgin olive oil until the pesto reaches your desired consistency. Season with salt and pepper to taste, and pulse a few more times to combine.
4. Once the pasta is cooked, drain it and return it to the pot. Add the pistachio pesto to the pasta and toss until evenly coated, adding a splash of pasta cooking water if needed to loosen the sauce.

5. Heat the pesto-coated pasta over low heat for a minute or two, stirring gently, to warm through.
6. Remove the pot from the heat and transfer the Fusilli with Pistachio Pesto to serving plates.
7. Optionally, garnish with additional grated Parmesan cheese and toasted pistachios for extra flavor and texture.
8. Serve hot and enjoy your delicious Fusilli with Pistachio Pesto, a flavorful and satisfying pasta dish with a unique twist!

www.ingramcontent.com/pod-product-compliance
Lightning Source LLC
LaVergne TN
LVHW061943070526
838199LV00060B/3948